MAGICAL BEANS A GIANT AND THE SCIENCE OF JACK AND THE BEANSTALK

WRITTEN BY MONICA CLARK-ROBINSON

ILLUSTRATED BY DANIEL WU

PICTURE WINDOW BOOKS
a capstone imprint

The SCIENTIFIC METHOD

1. Ask a Question
Ask yourself, "What do I want to learn more about?" or "I wonder what would happen if . . . ?"

2. Form a Hypothesis
Make a prediction or an educated guess about what might happen.

3. Experiment
Test your hypothesis by making a plan and conducting an experiment.

4. Observe and Record
Make careful observations during your experiment and write down what you see.

5. Analyze the Data
Collect and study the results of your data. Was your hypothesis correct?

6. Draw a Conclusion
Make your conclusion and share your results.

This is my home, where I live with my mother. And these are my animal friends.

Oh—and my name? Jack, of course. It's right there in the title.

I love science and animals. My cow, Moo-Bear, is my best friend.

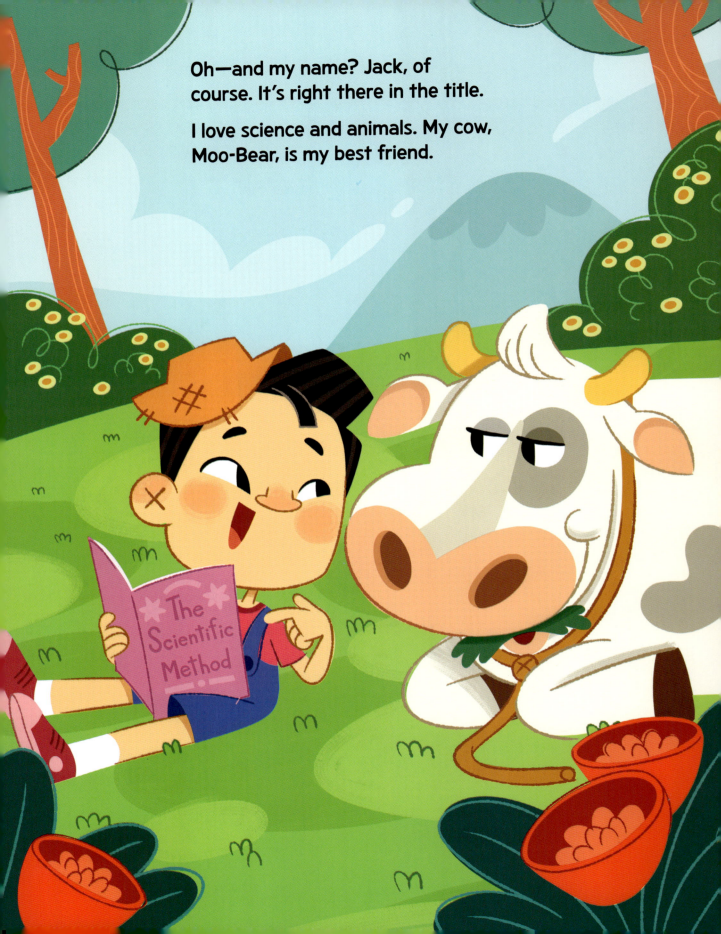

Then there's Mrs. Cluckworthy and Mrs. Pluckenduck.

I know what you're thinking. This story is called *Jack and the Beanstalk*, so where's the beanstalk?

Don't worry. That part's coming, and in a BIG way.

We aren't rich, but Mother always has ideas to help us get by. However, everything changed the day she had an idea I did _not_ like.

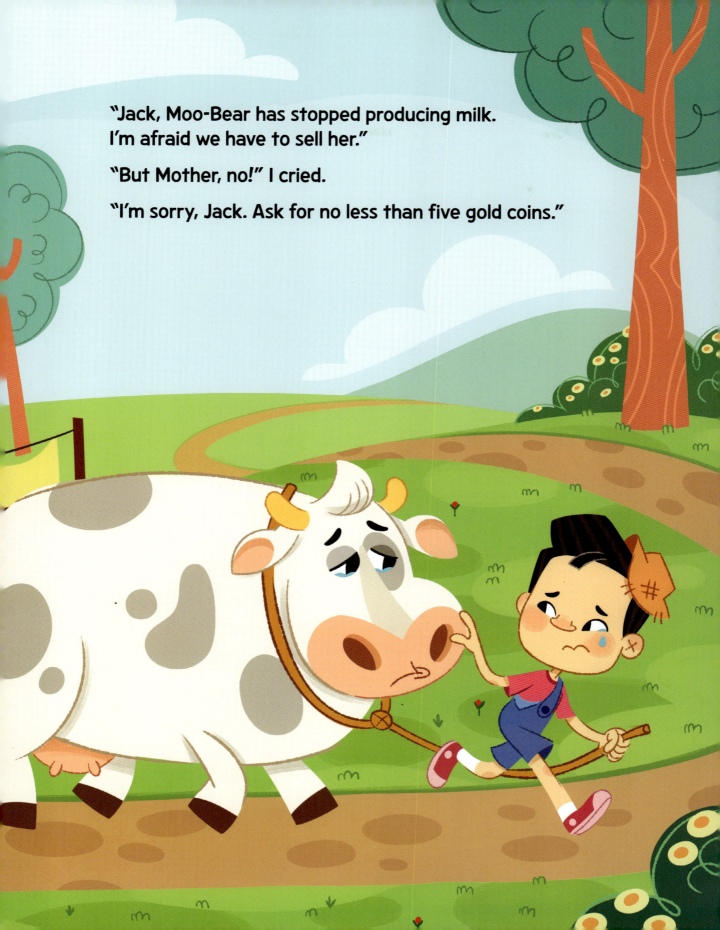

"Jack, Moo-Bear has stopped producing milk. I'm afraid we have to sell her."

"But Mother, no!" I cried.

"I'm sorry, Jack. Ask for no less than five gold coins."

At the market, a mysterious old man offered to buy Moo-Bear.

"My, what a fine cow!" he said. "I'll pay you five magic beans for her."

Magic beans sound pretty suspicious, I know. But I thought maybe something magical would happen and I could buy Moo-Bear back.

By the next morning, though, a giant beanstalk had grown into the sky.

Normal beanstalks don't grow this big—or this fast—do they? The beans *must* have been magic!

It was time for some science. I pulled a dried bean pod from the garden.

The scientific method always begins with a question.

QUESTION
Do all beanstalks grow overnight?

HYPOTHESIS
Beanstalks grow over months, not in one night.

EXPERIMENT
Plant a bean from a regular beanstalk and track its growth.

I planted the normal bean in a bucket
with some dirt and watered it.

I **OBSERVED** and **RECORDED** what I saw, then **ANALYZED** the data.

By the second day, my **CONCLUSION** was obvious. There was no sprout overnight. The beans from the market *must* have been magic!

Once my experiment was over,
it was time to climb!

I met a nice giantess in a castle above the clouds.
But she warned me about her husband.

He's a bit of a grump.
You probably want to head
home before he gets back.

I helped her with the dishes,

and she thanked me with a sack of gold to take home.

We had money for food and plenty left over to buy Moo-Bear back!
It was all just perfect. Until . . .

But this time, the grumpy giant was home. I had to be sneaky.

While I was looking for more coins, I saw a goose lay a golden egg! I couldn't resist THAT, and I definitely couldn't resist another animal friend!

I'll name you Mrs. Gigglegoose.

As I was leaving, I grabbed a golden harp for good measure.

I tiptoed out, but the giant's dog started barking. The giant woke up in a VERY bad mood.

With the giant chasing me, I began to worry. Would the beanstalk hold me while I was carrying so much extra weight?

Then I remembered that Mother made me do an experiment before I climbed the first time. She wanted to be sure the beanstalk would hold me.

We used the scientific method to find out.

QUESTION
Will the beanstalk hold my weight?

HYPOTHESIS
The beanstalk is so large it could hold someone twice my size.

EXPERIMENT
Test different sized objects on a thick branch to see if it will break.

We picked a tree with a branch that was similar in size to the beanstalk. I hung from the branch. It didn't bend.

Mother joined me. It still didn't bend!

And then, just for fun, all the animals joined in!
That's when the branch started to bend.

After we **ANALYZED** the data, Mother and I had our **CONCLUSION**.
The beanstalk was strong enough to hold someone twice as
big as me.

When the giant was halfway down, the beanstalk broke. He didn't have science on his side like I did.

I made it home safely, with money for medicine—and a sweet new pet.

The giantess let us keep the golden harp and Mrs. Gigglegoose, whose golden eggs helped us buy this new home. We planted the last of the magic beans so we can visit the giantess any time.

Now that you've heard my story and used the scientific method, would **YOU** have climbed the beanstalk?

FALLING OBJECTS EXPERIMENT

The heavy object (the giant) fell pretty fast from the beanstalk. I'm glad we didn't find out how fast the lighter object (me!) fell.

QUESTION
Do heavy or light objects fall faster?

HYPOTHESIS
Decide what your hypothesis will be and write it down.

EXPERIMENT
1. Choose at least three objects to drop. Make sure they are solid items that won't break, like a stuffed animal, a pencil, a crayon, a ruler, or a notebook.

NOTE: Do not use items like a piece of paper, a feather, a tissue, etc. The air resistance will slow them down, making your results incorrect.

2. Pick two of the objects, and carefully stand on top of a chair.

3. Hold your arms out at the same height, and drop the objects at the same time. **OBSERVE** what happens.

4. **RECORD** your data.

5. Do this until you've tested all the objects against each other.

6. **ANALYZE** your findings.

7. Draw your **CONCLUSION.** Was your hypothesis correct?

Meet the Author

Monica Clark-Robinson is passionately in love with the stories that connect us across culture, race, and age. She believes the right story, at the right time, can change a person's life. When not writing, Monica is a professional actor and voice-over artist and loves to cook and garden. She lives in a yurt in the country with one spouse, too many cats, and just the right amount of daughters.

photo credit: Domestika

Meet the Illustrator

Daniel Wu is a Brazilian illustrator who loves pizza, chocolate, and making people laugh. He fell in love with children's books as a kid and was amazed by the way they tell stories through pictures. He hasn't stopped drawing since. Daniel creates colorful, expressive characters full of life. His work can be found in games, magazines, and more. He lives in Germany, where he loves exploring Christmas markets.

Published by Picture Window Books, an imprint of Capstone
1710 Roe Crest Drive, North Mankato, Minnesota 56003
capstonepub.com

Library of Congress Cataloging-in-Publication Data is available on the Library of Congress website.
ISBN: 9798875216626 (hardcover)
ISBN: 9798875216572 (paperback)
ISBN: 9798875216589 (ebook PDF)

Summary: From magic beans to a massive beanstalk, Jack's story sounds questionable. He uses the scientific to try and prove that he is telling the truth.

Editor: Christianne Jones
Designer: Sarah Bennett
Production Specialist: Katy LaVigne

Printed and bound in China. 6274